MW01274985

IMAGES
of America

OLYMPIC MOUNTAINS

Port Townsend, 1901. On the eastern side of the Olympic Peninsula at the entrance to Puget Sound, Port Townsend was once the peninsula's largest city and the port for thousands of ships from all over the world. Much of its Victorian-era architecture is still in place.

On the Cover: Dungeness River Valley. The 32-mile-long Dungeness River begins high in the Olympic Mountains near Mystery Mountain and flows into Dungeness Bay on the Strait of Juan de Fuca. It is the second steepest river in the United States, dropping 7,300 feet over its length. In the upper reaches, it drops more than 1,000 feet per mile. The Dungeness River watershed includes 546 miles of streams and tributaries draining 172,517 acres. The river supports four species of salmon and ocean-going steelhead trout. Known as a "wild river," it changes course uncontrollably during flooding.

IMAGES
of America

OLYMPIC MOUNTAINS

Jefferson County Historical Society

ISBN 978-1-5316-5303-3

Published by Arcadia Publishing
Charleston, South Carolina

Library of Congress Control Number: 2009934871

For all general information contact Arcadia Publishing at:
Telephone 843-853-2070
Fax 843-853-0044
E-mail sales@arcadiapublishing.com
For customer service and orders:
Toll-Free 1-888-313-2665

Visit us on the Internet at www.arcadiapublishing.com

Contents

Acknowledgments		6
Introduction		7
1.	Rocks and Ice	9
2.	First People	17
3.	Water	23
4.	Newcomers	39
5.	Trees	61
6.	Recreation	79
7.	The Loop	107
Bibliography		127

Acknowledgments

The Jefferson County Historical Society (JCHS) maintains a fine collection of historical photographs. The society sincerely thanks all who have donated to this collection and encourages anyone with images that illustrate the history of the Olympic Peninsula to add to this resource.

Photographers Paul M. Richardson, George Welch, William H. Wilcox, James G. McCurdy, Sanford Lake, and many others took wonderful photographs documenting the history of the Olympic Peninsula. Without their skill, enthusiasm, and willingness to pack in cumbersome photography equipment we would not have these images.

Jefferson County Historical Society volunteers continue to scan and index the photograph collection. Many thanks to Lillian Raines, Rex Rice, Stan White, Arthur C. D. Cannon, Shane Miller, Roman Meza, Catherine Garrison, and Alan Hughes. Victoria Davis and Jim Christenson keep the computer software and hardware updated and in working order. JCHS archivist Marsha Moratti chose the photographs and wrote the text. Marge Samuelson and Winona Prill checked the historical facts. Steve Ricketts provided historical information on logging. Catherine Garrison and Peggy Harju provided their excellent editing and proofreading skills.

All images are from the collection of the Jefferson County Historical Society.

INTRODUCTION

The Olympic Mountains remain elemental. Rocks, water, sky, flora, and fauna abide in unspoiled abundance. The Pacific Ocean roars in, pounding against sea stacks and sandy beaches. Misty cool air becomes a deluge of rain as clouds rise and encounter the mountain barrier. This rain nurtures a green world photosynthesizing with abandon.

Higher up, the rain falls as snow. Glaciers—still here from the last ice age—build a seasonal snowpack. The spring melt reveals alpine meadows of wildflowers and fuels a watershed of creeks and rivers that flow into lakes and the surrounding ocean, strait, and fjord. Bodies of water surround the Olympic Peninsula on three sides, providing enough isolation to allow distinct species to evolve and thrive. The creeks, streams, and rivers link the ocean and land ecosystems. Ocean-going salmon return and swim upstream to spawn in the creeks where they hatched. There they die, bringing nutrients from the ocean to feed everything springing up from the spongy forest floor. Thriving here are elk, bear, deer, cougar, and hundreds of smaller creatures, many found only on the Olympic Peninsula.

Humans were late to arrive here. Archeologists have found hunting camps of Native Americans deep in the mountains but no permanent settlements. Like the settlers who started arriving in the 1850s, natives lived on the coastal waters and in the river valleys.

Traditionally the Chimacum, Hoh, S'Klallam, Quinault, Snohomish, and Twana tribes lived on the Olympic Peninsula. By the late 1700s, these people had been devastated by contact with European diseases. In 1854, Pres. Franklin Pierce gave Isaac I. Stevens the triple role of Washington territorial governor, Indian agent, and chief railroad surveyor. Stevens implemented the government's paternalistic policy of removing native people to reservations. The intent was to protect Native Americans from conflict with settlers and to create an environment where they could be "civilized." The prevailing sentiment of the time was that through schooling and conversion to Christianity, Native Americans would be suitable for assimilation into American society. Stevens negotiated 10 treaties, including two that covered the Olympic Peninsula's Makah, Quileute, Hoh, Queets, and Quinault tribes. Treaties established two reservations: one at Neah Bay and another north of Grays Harbor at Point Greenville. Today the Hoh, Quinault, and Makah live on reservations on the Pacific Ocean coast.

European and American immigrants began to settle on the Olympic Peninsula in the mid-19th century, situating in villages at easily accessible, deep-water bays. While a few adventurous settlers chose property inland for homesteading, most activity was concentrated along the coastline, where seafood was abundant and boats of all sizes transported people and goods. There were no roads through the dense forests.

In 1862, Congress passed new provisions under the Homestead Act whereby U.S. citizens—or immigrants intending to become citizens—could claim 160 acres of public land. Married couples could claim 320 acres. Once claims were made, settlers were required to live on the land for five years and make certain improvements. Qualifying improvements included building living quarters and clearing land for farming. The provisions of the Homestead Act were not suited to conditions on the Olympic Peninsula. Massive old-growth forests, steep terrain, rain forests, and rocky coastlines made clearing enough land to fulfill the terms of the law a daunting assignment.

The forests did not yield way to become bountiful farmlands as in other regions. The average farm was small and often swamped by too much rain and flooding rivers and streams. Still, many courageous, optimistic, and hardworking settlers carved clearings out of the vast wilderness.

Would-be farmers first worked as loggers, both to clear their own land and to earn money to make improvements on their claims. Men took jobs as loggers, mill hands, and timber cruisers. There were some government jobs—mail carriers, surveyors, and forest rangers. Some also worked as miners, commercial fishers, bounty hunters, packers, or on road construction crews. Meanwhile, their wives and children worked the farms.

As soon as gold was discovered in California in 1849 there was a market for timber from the Puget Sound region. By the mid-1850s, investors had built dozens of sawmills. Timber quickly became the major export and provided a seemingly inexhaustible resource on which to base the local economy. As forests near water were logged off, timber-harvesting methods became more innovative. In the 1880s, teams of oxen and skid roads gave way to steam-powered donkey engines and railroads. Narrow-gauge logging railroads provided an efficient means of moving logs out of deep woods. High-lead loggers suspended logs through the air instead of dragging them along the ground, making it possible to cut trees on steep slopes and in narrow valleys. Predictably, moving huge logs through the air above workers' heads was frequently deadly. Gasoline-powered chainsaws were a vast improvement over axes and crosscut saws, and were in use by the start of World War II. By the early 1960s, log trucks had replaced the logging railroads.

The conflict between those who would cut trees and those who would preserve the forests is long-standing and ongoing. Early conservationists advocated for preserving much of the beautiful Olympic Peninsula. Homesteading and logging interests had powerful political advocates, but in 1897, Pres. Grover Cleveland created the Olympic Forest Reserve. Congress declared the area a national monument in 1909 and a national park in 1938. This shift generated backlashes along the way where more lands were temporarily apportioned to logging and homesteading. It was never enough to assure settlers that their efforts would not ultimately be in vain. In 1897, more than half of the homesteaders affected by the new reserve status sold or abandoned their claims. The extension of the Olympic National Park in 1953 to a portion of the western coast forced yet more homesteaders to give up their land. Logging, although reduced in scope, remains an important industry on the Olympic Peninsula.

The popularity of hiking, camping, fishing, and other outdoor recreation grew as automobiles and roads made the backcountry accessible. Those logging the national forests and organizations devoted to enjoying the wilderness were increasingly at odds. After a long campaign, environmental groups successfully pushed the Wilderness Act through Congress in 1964. This bill allowed for some federal lands to receive a wilderness designation that prohibited all forms of development except the construction of hiking trails. The passage of the Endangered Species Act in 1973 was another environmentalist victory. The law required the U.S. Fish and Wildlife Service to identify threatened plants and animals, and to take actions to promote their recovery.

Eventually these new environmental protections shut down logging in 65 percent of the Olympic National Forest. For many who lived and worked in logging communities, it was the end of an era. Many found other ways to make a living. Communities began to promote tourism, lauding the beautiful parks and charming communities. They continue to feature educational programs, festivals, farmers' markets, and arts events while encouraging the construction of new parks, resorts, restaurants, and inns. These tourism-based jobs do not replace the incomes once earned by logging and mill work; many families have moved away.

The shift from logging to tourism brought more indoor, outdoor, and year-round offerings for both residents and visitors. There is much to enjoy on the Olympic Peninsula, and it has become an increasingly attractive place for retirees and world travelers.

One

Rocks and Ice

Millions of years ago, geologic forces under the Pacific Ocean caused vents, fissures, and lava flows to create huge underwater seamounts. The plates that formed the ocean floor went beneath the continental landmass. Portions of the sea floor were scraped off and jammed against the mainland, creating the dome that was the forerunner of today's Olympic Mountains. The jagged rock-pile appearance of these mountains is the result of powerful forces fracturing, folding, and jumbling formations over time.

Ice age glacial sheets from the north carved out the Strait of Juan de Fuca and Puget Sound, isolating the Olympics from nearby landmasses. This created a coastal refuge. Radiating out from the center of the dome—Mount Olympus—snow, rain, creeks, and rivers carved steep slopes, creating a beautiful, rugged landscape.

The Olympic Mountains were not explored by non-natives until the late 19th century, beginning with U.S. Army expeditions. Lt. Joseph P. O'Neil was impressed by the views of snow-covered mountains rising in "wild, broken confusion." He picked out what he thought was Olympus, the crowning point in a range that appeared to circle on itself. "There is no regularity about their formation," he wrote of the Olympics in general, "but jumbled up in the utmost confusion and the only regularity which does exist is that the ranges nearest the Strait and Sound seem to run parallel to those bodies of water." He predicted that the day would come when the future State of Washington would "glory in their wealth and beauty." Lieutenant O'Neil, who went on to become a brigadier general, lived to see his wish come true. On June 29, 1938, four weeks prior to his death, Congress created Olympic National Park, nearly a half century after he had proposed it.

Steep Slope in the Olympics. The Olympic range is a compact cluster of peaks that are not especially high but are steep and rugged. Snowfields and glaciers surround the higher peaks; wild rivers have carved out canyons.

Mount Olympus. At 7,965 feet, the jagged crest of Mount Olympus is the highest point in Olympic National Park. It was named by English sea captain John Meares on July 4, 1778, when he viewed it from his ship in the Pacific Ocean. The mountain was originally called *Sun-a-do* by the Duwamish Indians. In 1774, the Spanish named it *Cero Nevada de Santa Rosalia.* It receives more than 200 inches of precipitation a year, mostly in the form of snow.

Mount Anderson. Centrally located in the range, the west peak of Anderson's summit is the hydrographic apex of the Olympic Peninsula. Water from this point drains into the Pacific Ocean, Hood Canal, and the Strait of Juan de Fuca. Mount Anderson was named in 1885 by Lt. Joseph O'Neal in honor of his commanding officer, Maj. Gen. Thomas H. Anderson. It rises to 7,321 feet.

Out from Bald Mountain. This image is from a postcard postmarked Port Townsend, November 1, 1914. The message reads: "Dear Bro: One we took the last time out from Bald Mountain. You see we had some snow for sure, but good weather and views galore. Paul" Paul M. Richardson was an accomplished photographer and outdoorsman who left behind many glorious images of the Olympics.

Ice Lake, East of Mount Angeles. The view from the summit of Mount Angeles provides a grand vista into the heart of the range, including Mount Olympus to the southwest and north across the Strait of Juan de Fuca to the city of Victoria on Vancouver Island.

Summer Mountainsides. Wind, cold, and heavy snow make life challenging for mountain trees. The subalpine forest is a transition zone from the dense forest below to alpine tundra above. Trees gradually get smaller and more stunted higher up a mountain. The tree line in the Olympics lies between 5,000 and 6,000 feet.

AN OLYMPIC GLACIER. There are about 266 glaciers crowning the Olympic peaks. The most prominent are those on Mount Olympus, covering approximately 10 square miles. Beyond the Olympic complex are the glaciers of Mount Carrie, the Bailey Range, Mount Christie, and Mount Anderson.

MOUNT CONSTANCE. The highest and most massive peak on the eastern front of the Olympics, Mount Constance is the fifth-highest peak in the range after Mount Deception and the three summits of Mount Olympus. In 1857, Lt. George Davidson anchored his ship in a cove in Puget Sound. Impressed with the spectacular view of the Olympics to the west, he named Mount Ellinor for his bride-to-be. He also named the Brothers, Mount Constance, and Mount Rose for members of his future family.

CANOE WITH SAIL. From spring until late fall, small family groups of Native Americans were scattered along the coast, especially at the many river outlets where seasonal salmon runs provided a winter's worth of fish to smoke and dry. Canoes are traditionally made of a single cedar log that is hollowed out and shaped with simple tools, skilled hands, and a spirit helper. They remain vital to the cultural heritage of the Northwest Coast native people.

BASKET WEAVER "ELSA" AT LAPUSH. Most of the natives' material needs were met using products of the cedar tree and other plants: canoes and cedar-plank houses, steam-bent boxes and implements, elaborate baskets, hats and mats, nets, cords, and woven cloth of cedar-bark fiber. According to a 1930s book entitled *Where-to-Go, Directory of the Pacific Coast*, the home of the Quileute Indians, "LaPush is an interesting Indian village on the Pacific Coast, where one can go by boat or foot from the settlement of Mora."

Two

FIRST PEOPLE

When European explorers first sailed along the coast of what is now Washington State, people had been living beside the rivers, lakes, bays, and beaches of the Olympic Peninsula for nearly 12,000 years. Food was plentiful, the weather mild, and travel easy by canoe. During the dark, wet winters, they told stories, carved wood and bone, and wove baskets, creating rich traditions. Historically, several groups of Coast Salish had permanent winter lodges on Olympic Peninsula coasts, including the Klallam/S'Klallam (Clallam); the related Quileute, Hoh, and Chemakum (Chimakum); the Twana-related Kilsid (Quilcene); and the related Quinault and Queets. They were joined by other groups in the summer months, notably the Nootka-related Makah from Cape Flattery, as all nomadically pursued the abundant coastal resources.

By the late 1700s, these people had been devastated by contact with European diseases. In 1855, in the Point No Point Treaty and the Quinault River Treaty, the tribes ceded their lands to the United States. Today the Hoh, Quinault, and Makah people live on reservation lands bordered by the spectacular Pacific coastline. The Jamestown S'Klallams purchased property near Dungeness in 1874.

James G. Swan arrived in the frontier settlement of Port Townsend early in 1859. He had a uniquely profound, empathetic interest in the natives. His prolific writings provide insight into the ways of the Native Americans and their struggle to adapt to a rapidly changing world:

> I know the character of the coast Indians so well . . . I have been with them so much, and so long, that I feel perfectly safe with them, at times too, when the least betrayal of fear would lose for me that respect and confidence they now repose in me. The secret of my success with these people is in the rule I always follow. I never tell an Indian a lie, even in a joke, and I have never since I have been in this Territory, which is since 1852, carried a weapon of defense with me whenever I went among them. I have always found that a civil tongue is the best weapon I can use.

NINA BRIGHT AT NEAH BAY. A woman who needed to make baskets began planning many months in advance. Basketry was primarily winter work, but the materials were gathered in the summer. Roots and twigs were soaked, peeled, and split; grass was cured and sometimes dyed. One native woman said, "When I begin to weave a basket, my work is already half done."

NATIVE WOMEN OUTSIDE CABIN. Native tribes of the region were generally friendly and cooperative, providing help to settlers with transportation and labor. Homesteader Hulda Sullivan Nylund recalled that the Ozette Indians, who were always friendly, traveled by canoe up the Ozette River from their village to Eagle Point, where they caught, dried, and smoked salmon. "They built big bonfires and held powwows far into the night, beating their drums and chanting," she said.

Basket Makers at Kalaloch, August 1881. The art of basket making was highly developed by native women throughout Washington State. Different types of baskets were used for cooking, food gathering and storage, and carrying water. Colored grasses, which were the native woman's version of embroidery silks, were among her most valued possessions. Basket makers embellished their work with fancy edges and many varieties of stitches.

Woman in a Canoe. Dense forests and rough terrain made travel nearly impossible by land. Canoes were used for visiting other villages and moving from winter homes to summer camps. Fishing and collecting shellfish, sea vegetables, and seabird eggs required canoes.

Canoe Rigged for Sailing. According to the writings of James G. Swan in *The Indians of Cape Flattery*, "Formerly mats were used as canoe sails, but at present they are employed for wrapping up blankets, for protecting the cargoes in canoes, and for sale to the whites, who use them as lining of rooms or floor coverings."

Fishing for Halibut. According to the writings of James G. Swan in *San Francisco Evening Bulletin*, dated September 1859, "Their fishing lines and whale gear are made of stems of the gigantic kelp found on our coast, which grows from 40 to 50 feet in length. These stems are stretched and rubbed to make them of uniform size, and then kept knotted together to form the required line. This kelp is very strong and serves every purpose for these Indians instead of hemp or flaxen cords."

VILLAGE AT CHIMACUM CREEK. The following quote was taken from an oral history of William Edward Matheson in 1989: "Chimacum Creek was one of the best fishing streams on the peninsula, and in the fertile valley there were many large beaver dams. There were also large crabapple groves, and the prairie in Chimacum was a feeding ground for deer and elk. Berries were abundant everywhere. Clams and mussels were also very abundant on the miles of waterfront. . . . It's not difficult to see why so many Snohomish Indian families settled in this area."

CHILDREN AT NEAH BAY. James G. Swan taught in the Native American school here. Swan was a rarity among early Washington settlers—he was fascinated by native culture. Swan first visited Neah Bay in March 1859. For the next three years, he traveled often between Port Townsend and the Makah reservation at Neah Bay, often in Makah canoes. By the fall of 1861, Swan was living in Neah Bay. He traveled on foot to all five Makah villages—Neah and Baada on the strait, and Sooes, Waatch, and Ozette on the Pacific Coast—to conduct the first census of the Makah, counting a total of 654 tribal members. He was appointed schoolteacher and supervised the construction of a schoolhouse and other Indian agency buildings. He spent the next four years living in the schoolhouse and teaching when he could persuade children to attend. Swan respected the Makah culture enough to not force school on them.

Cape Flattery, Three Sisters Rocks. At the entrance to the Strait of Juan de Fuca, this high, rocky bluff on the Makah Indian Reservation overlooks Tatoosh Island and the Pacific Ocean. Charted by Capt. James Cook of the British Navy on March 22, 1778, Cape Flattery is the oldest name now in use on maps of Washington State. Captain Cook chose it because the cape flattered him with the hope of a passage between it and the island beyond, which was Vancouver Island. Because of bad weather Cook failed to find the Strait of Juan de Fuca.

Ocean Meets Hoh River. The Olympic Coast National Marine Sanctuary encompasses about 135 miles of pristine coastline and 2,500 square nautical miles. The sanctuary protects one of the largest concentrations of seabirds in the continental United States, more varieties of kelp than anywhere else, and the world's largest octopus species. It is the home of transplanted sea otters and provides a haven for gray whales migrating south and north in fall and spring. Seals, sea lions, deer, and eagles are common sights among the sea stacks and tiny islands that surging surf has pounded out of the coastline over the ages.

Three

Water

Seldom is the word "sea" used to describe any of the waters surrounding the Olympic Peninsula. Creeks and rivers flow from the glaciers of the Olympic Mountains, coursing into the Pacific Ocean, the Strait of Juan de Fuca, Puget Sound, and Hood Canal. These more specific definitions are needed to make sense of such a watery place. The ocean, the strait, the sound, and the canal all describe places with wildly varying characteristics. The ocean here is turbulent, as can be the strait. The inland sound and canal are calmer but certainly not always. Residents are even more specific—Upper Hoh, Cape Flattery, Quilcene Bay, Dosewallips. All of these waters constantly sculpt away the land.

From a small airplane it is easy to see that the jagged peaks of the Olympic Mountains have shorter brothers and sisters submerged under some of these waters. Ebb and flow tides move massive amounts of water through underwater mountain ranges, sand spits, mudflats, and shoals to create swirling, churning, choppy, and fast-flowing currents.

The Olympics intercept moisture-rich air masses moving in from the Pacific Ocean. As this air rises over the mountains, it cools and releases moisture in the form of rain or snow. Precipitation ranges from 140 to 220 inches, (12 to 18 feet), every year. At lower elevations rain nurtures the forests, while at higher elevations snow adds to glacial masses. The mountains wring precipitation out of the air so effectively that areas on the northeast corner of the peninsula are in a rain shadow, receiving little precipitation. Only 17 inches a year fall on the town of Sequim, while less than 30 miles away Mount Olympus receives more than 220 inches, falling mostly as snow. The misty West End is the wettest place in the 48 contiguous states. This moisture-rich temperate rain forest provides an abundant habitat for many unique species of plants and animals.

Elwha River Canyon. During an era of reckless economic optimism, two hydropower dams were built on the Elwha River. These dams, which generate little power, have virtually destroyed the Elwha River's rich fish runs and have completely disrupted the economic and social life of the Elwha tribe. The Olympic Power Company began construction of the first dam in 1910. In 1927, Northwestern Power and Light Company completed a second dam, the Glines Canyon Dam. Like the Elwha Dam, it was not equipped with fish-passage facilities.

Lower Elwha Dam. In 1912, as the reservoir filled behind the nearly-completed dam, the lower sections gave way, and a torrent of water headed downstream, taking out a bridge. Rebuilt in 1913, the dam still lacked passage for migrating salmon, blocking the upper 68 miles of river habitat. Salmon runs that once numbered more than 400,000 now number less than 4,000. Dam removal is scheduled to begin in 2012.

Log Bridge across Quilcene River. As a wilderness park, much of the interior of the Olympics is accessible only by trail. Bridges are handmade from the abundant trees.

CROSSING THE ELWHA RIVER. Before bridges and dams, this was one way to cross a wide spot in the river.

Leland Lake and Olympic Mountains. At one time there were three lumber mills at the lake. It was a source for lumber during the boom years in Port Townsend.

Postcard from the Hoh River. The message on the back reads, "Dear Kate, Here is a canoe landing on the lower Hoh River . . . We stayed here for several days and from this place had the greatest canoe ride down the river to the ocean that I ever expect to have, Paul." Paul Richardson took many photographs of his adventures in the Olympics.

Boating on Lake Crescent, c. 1915. The Lake Crescent Lodge, built in 1916, attracted visitors to this lovely lake. It is the only remaining resort from the lake's boom days and was once visited by Pres. Franklin D. Roosevelt. In the mid-1930s, twelve resorts dotted the lake. Auto camps sprang up in the 1940s and 1950s. Beardslee Bay Camp, Lenoir's East Beach, Log Cabin, Bonnie Brae, and LaPoel and Julius Peterson's resort served the auto-touring visitors.

View of Lake Crescent. The 12-mile-long lake stands out like an alpine gem embedded in a steep, mountain setting. The most popular lake sights and activities include swimming and sunbathing at East Beach and the hike from Storm King Ranger Station to the 90-foot Marymere Falls. The lake is legendary for its Beardslee trout, a landlocked fish that resembles a steelhead but is unique to Lake Crescent.

Box Canyon, Hoh River. The Hoh is a glacier melt river: it is colder and often higher in summer and warmer in the winter when fed by rainfall. Note the people on the cliff.

CROSSING THE QUINAULT RIVER. In the fall a winter's worth of supplies needed to be brought in to the remote homesteads before the heavy rains came. Crossing rivers would be even more difficult in the spring and summer as snow was melting.

FORDING THE RIVER. Finding a safe place to cross the many twists and turns in the rivers could be a challenge. Many homesteaders never learned to swim; the idea was to stay out of the glacier-fed waters.

AGAINST THE STREAM. Ben Northup and an unidentified friend poled a canoe up the Clearwater River. As difficult as this appears, it was easier than hauling supplies over rugged slopes. It would take half a day to get down river and three days to get back home upriver. Northup was an expert canoe handler and supported his family by providing ferry service and fishing tours on the Clearwater and Queets Rivers.

Lake Sutherland. There is a legend that Mount Storm King became angry at warring Clallam and Quileute tribes—so angry that he threw down a massive rock, dividing Lake Crescent from Lake Sutherland. Geologists believe that the lakes were formed 8,000 years ago and became separated by a massive landslide.

Wading in Quilcene Bay. Hood Canal beaches warm up a little more than other saltwater beaches. This 45-mile, north-to-south body of water is not actually a canal but a natural fjord.

Pleasant Harbor, Brinnon. Pleasant Harbor is a protected, deep-water harbor on the west side of Hood Canal on Highway 101.

Overview of Hood Canal. Hood Canal was named by Royal Navy captain George Vancouver for Admiral Lord Samuel Hood on May 13, 1792. Vancouver used the name "Hood's Channel" in his journal, but "Hood's Canal" on his charts. The U.S. Geographic Board decided on "Hood Canal" as the official name in 1932. Technically Hood Canal is a fjord.

Launch and Wharf. It was common practice to get groceries by sending an order with the captain of a boat that was running supplies back and forth. A boat captain could earn a good living moving people and provisions around since the only alternative was walking on trails through the woods.

WHARF AT NEAH BAY, 1919. Today the fishing village of Neah Bay is the heart of the Makah Nation. A new marina safely harbors more than 200 boats. The renowned Makah Museum allows visitors to explore the lifestyle of pre-contact Makah people.

DOCK AT PORT WILLIAMS. Once located on the Strait of Juan de Fuca, this town was named for a contractor who tried to promote the town site in the 1890s. According to Florence A. Merriam in her 1889 account, *A Tugboat Trip to the Northwest Corner*, "The semiweekly visit of the tugboat was evidently the event of the hamlets along the straits. Even the schoolchildren came to see it, with their dinner pails on their arms."

River Transport, 1922. The *Olympic* towed spruce logs out of the Hoh Rain Forest to be sold for spruce veneer.

Ocean Steamer. Ocean-going ships brought the bulk of West End homesteaders' supplies from Port Townsend. At high tide, the large steam ships would be unloaded at the mouth of a river.

Ocean-Going Canoe. Larger than hunting canoes, ocean canoes have a carved head in the bow that appears to be looking out to sea. Native canoes were quickly adopted by settlers as an excellent way to get around and could be purchased from the Native Americans for about $25.

A Ship in Port Townsend Bay. Surrounded on three sides by water, Port Townsend was a shipping hub during a time when the transportation of nearly all people and goods depended upon sea travel.

DONALIA FREY AND BEAR. The Freys lived in the Brinnon area. In the 1930s, they owned and operated the Maples grocery and filling station. Donalia Frey's first husband, Bob Kenney, drowned when he tried to cross the flooding Dosewallips River after the bridge washed out. Kenney, along with his team and wagon, were never found.

Four

Newcomers

In the mid-1800s, free land for homesteading brought people from around the world to the Olympic Peninsula. Under the Homestead Act of 1862, an individual could claim 160 acres (320 acres for a married couple) of public land for a small fee. Homesteaders received title to their land if they lived on it continuously and made certain improvements within five years, known as "proving up." Newspapers, the government, railroad companies, and land speculators encouraged emigration. With its vast natural resources, unsurpassed scenery, mild temperatures, and plentiful rainfall, the Olympic Peninsula was lauded as a farmer's paradise. What early settlers actually found were huge trees and no roads or marketplaces. Few crops would grow because of poor drainage, rivers prone to flooding, and a short growing season. Most homesteaders kept a few animals and, along with the plentiful wild carnivores, hunted deer and elk and fished the streams. In the west part of the peninsula, the forest was always in the process of reclaiming the land. Grazing cattle helped to keep the land clear.

On the West End, homesteading was generally a temporary endeavor. Even for those few remaining farmers willing and able to face the hardships, there was the early and abiding presence of the Olympic Forest Reserve, established in 1897. Uncertainty about the future of the region made homesteaders less willing to invest their lives on a claim that might prove worthless. Many old claims and homesteads were, indeed, absorbed by the Olympic National Park when it was established in 1938.

A few families stayed on, but most upland settlers sold their property to timber companies and moved to the more fertile valleys. On the eastern side of the mountains, markets were closer and urban centers were just a steamship ride away. On cleared land settlers grew clovers, timothy, hops, fruit trees, wheat, oats, berries, and root crops. Dairy farms proved to be the most successful and enduring agricultural operations in the area.

EMMA OLSON WASHING CLOTHES. Homesteads in Brinnon were accessible only via the waters of the Hood Canal. Cabins dotted the steep riverbanks where women and children worked to "prove up" the farm while men worked in the logging camps.

G. W. AND MATILDA EDWARDS, LELAND. According to Lillie Christiansen's account of her childhood near here in the 1890s, meals were often white bread, beans, potatoes, and lard gravy. Every household had a hunting gun, but because of the many wild predators, venison was relatively scarce.

KAICHI KAWAMOTO FAMILY, 1910. Kaichi Kawamoto immigrated to America from Japan in 1898. He worked for nine years at railroad and lumber jobs. After he settled in Leland Valley, his wife, Itsuno, joined him in 1906. The baby is Jeanette (Yoneko), and the boy is Joseph.

Quilcene Post Office. At first, mail service was from the mill town of Seabeck whenever Quilcene residents went by boat to call for it. In some communities, the post offices were moved from house to house of anyone willing to serve as postmaster. The Irondale, Leland, Quileute, and Quilcene Post Offices were all established in 1881. After that, a mail boat made deliveries three times a week from Port Townsend to Port Discovery, where Quilcene's mail was picked up for delivery by horseback.

THE MEGAPHONE PRINTING SHOP. *The Megaphone* was a weekly newspaper and print shop situated next to a stream flowing from Mount Walker into a Hood Canal bay. The first issue of *The Megaphone* was dated July 17, 1909. A huge waterwheel powered the press. The editor, Milton F. Satterlee, was "one of the biggest jokers in the State of Washington," according to the special correspondent for the *American Forester Review* in March 1915. Prior to publishing *The Megaphone*, Satterlee was the editor and publisher of the *Quilcene Queen*.

FRANK FLEISHMAN'S CABIN, C. 1910. Fleishman homesteaded on Cedar Creek on the Upper Hoh River. Until 1890, there was no serious effort to settle in the Olympic Mountains and the rain forest of the Hoh River watershed. Clearing underbrush and larger trees was the primary and ongoing objective. Settlers burned large logs, and branches and smaller logs became firewood. Split cedar and spruce provided shakes for cabins and outbuildings.

Hoh River Settlers. Pictured from left to right are (first row) Pete Willowby, Coper Land, Karl Fischer, John Fletcher, Henery Huelsdonk, and unidentified; (second row) John Huelsdonk, Pete Brandeberry, Fred Fletcher, Roy Smith, Fred Fischer, and Jim Reed.

Stump Farming. Clearing the land of trees was an arduous task. Many loggers felled the large trees the native way, by drilling holes in the base of the tree and dropping in live coals. A bellows and lung power kept the fire going. After the tree burned enough to fall, it was either cut up or burned, and the big remaining stump was burned, dug, and pried from the ground. Millions of board feet of fine timber were burned by homesteaders to clear land for farming.

LAUBACH HOMESTEAD ON DISCOVERY BAY. Homesteaders began "proving up" their claims by building small cabins, planting gardens, and putting up sheds and barns for their animals. They then set about clearing land to grow crops. Cutting down the trees was difficult and dangerous; removing stumps a huge endeavor, almost unimaginable today.

STURROCK AND MUNN FAMILIES, 1897. Those pictured were identified by Hector John Munn Jr. as Clara Sturrock (with parasol); James Hector Munn with his dog, Bruno; Mary Sturrock (daughter of Mr. and Mrs. George Sturrock); Nellie Lumsden; Willie Lumsden (standing); Hector John Munn, age 9, (child sitting); Mrs. James H. (Ana M.) Munn (sitting); Alice Margaret Munn; and Viola Munn. The Sturrock family was in the area assisting Jim Munn with the construction of a sawmill. George Sturrock was a millwright.

Sheep Grazing on a Bluff. Rocky soils were more suitable for grazing than farming. Lake Ozette homesteader Johanna Nylund kept a flock of sheep and spun wool. She knitted and crocheted the yarn into caps, sweaters, socks, and undergarments ideal for the rainy climate.

Mother and Daughter Knitting. Vendla Martinsen and Mary Martinsen are pictured knitting in the front yard of their Brinnon homestead around 1916.

Phillip Dahm Farm. The farmer and his ox team are pictured here near Discovery Bay.

Home on Steamboat Creek. Most West End homesteaders kept a few farm animals. A sturdy fence and dog could help keep out the wild carnivores. One settler lost a whole herd of goats, one at a time, when the bears found them tasty.

Berry Picking. From left to right are Myrtle Neyhart and her neighbor Mary Martinsen. Myrtle was nine years old when she arrived in Brinnon with her parents, Frank and Mary Neyhart. She spent most of her life in Brinnon, except for a stint working for the telephone company in Seattle when she was a young woman.

Walter Martinsen in a Buggy. The horse was named Buster. The widowed Vendla Roselle brought three children—Ernest, Elof, and Eleanor—into her marriage to Otto Martinsen. The couple had four more children: Andrew, Harry, Mary, and Walter.

Mr. and Mrs. Martinsen's Wedding Portrait. Capt. Otto Martinsen married Vendla Roselle in January 1902. For many years, Martinsen tried his hand at farming on the Brinnon homestead before returning to work on the water as a tugboat captain.

Haying on the Old Homestead, 1917. The Roselle and Martinson children often returned to the Brinnon homestead to help harvest the hay crop.

MABEL WITH HER FATHER. E. C. Adams and his daughter Mabel enjoy a summer day in the orchard of their Quilcene home.

FARMER FEEDING HIS TURKEYS. John Huelsdonk once contracted Mickey Merchant, usually a logger and prospector, to drive a flock of turkeys over the Hoh-Bogachiel Trail to market in Forks.

Lindstrom Farm on Discovery Bay. The Carl and Ida Lindstrom family, originally from Sweden, farmed in the area from 1907 until they moved to Seattle in 1928.

Haying Near Quilcene. Farmers cut hay by hand with a scythe and then raked and hauled it by sled to the barn. Even after the children grew up and left for the "outside," they tried to come home during haying time to help.

School at Quilcene. Children went to primary and secondary schools if they were available. Most settlements built fine school buildings.

Dunning Family of Quilcene. The Dunning family moved to Quilcene around 1885. There were seven children in the family, with Kate, the youngest, born in a log house on the 360-acre homestead. Kate recalled that the family lived quite far away from stores, so they ordered their shoes from Port Townsend, a 26-mile, two-day trip by horse and buggy. The parents drew patterns of the children's feet on paper. Kate loved to go to Port Townsend and run up and down the halls of the huge, new courthouse. (The building is still in use.) She lived in Quilcene until she was 17 and completed two years of high school before moving to Seattle.

KATE BRINNON IN HER GARDEN, 1916. In the 1860s, Elwell P. Brinnon and his Klallam wife, Kate, homesteaded at the mouth of the Duckabush River. Soon after, they moved to the Dosewallips River area. By the 1880s, the Brinnons owned most of the property in the lower Dosewallips Valley and gave much of it to the community that now bears their name.

Harry Brown's Cattle. Farmland was irrigated (and frequently flooded) by glacier-fed creeks, allowing cattle to graze year-round. At one time, almost every farm family had a small herd of cows. Although dairy farms proved to be the most successful and enduring agricultural operations in the area, few are still in operation. The February 16, 1931, edition of the *Port Townsend Leader* reported that the Chimacum Valley was home to 28 dairy farms.

Dunning's Cherry Orchard. The Dunnings raised livestock and grew grain. Like many other homesteaders, they planted large vegetable gardens and orchards of fruit trees. Blackberries, raspberries, currants, gooseberries, and strawberries grew especially well in the fertile soil. Potatoes were a mainstay crop.

LOWER HOH SCHOOL, 1906. From left to right are John R. Fletcher, Myrtle Anderson, Lulu Anderson (standing), Grace Baker Fletcher (teacher), Nellie (Helen) Anderson (right of teacher), and Nansen Anderson. In 1968, the schoolhouse was moved 600 feet back from the shore to avoid being flooded by the Hoh River.

SECOND BRINNON SCHOOL. This log schoolhouse was built in 1894 on the same site as the current school on land donated by Ewell and Kate Brinnon. Pictured from left to right are (first row) Addie Macomber, Zola Kinney, Katie Macomber, Romie Jameson, Ira Macomber, Guy Robinson, and Earl Robinson; (second row) Neva Kinney, Daisy Macomber, Bert Macomber, Will Warin (not a pupil), Pluma Kinney (Mrs. C. R. Thomas), and Joe Boshambro (on horse). The first Brinnon school was established on May 2, 1881, at the head of Pleasant Harbor.

Mrs. Biles and Deer. Throughout the year, deer are found in nearly every habitat of the Olympic Peninsula, from the Pacific beaches, to high-country meadows, to anyone's backyard.

T. B. Balch Family, Brinnon. True D. Balch was born on the Quillayute prairie near Forks in 1889. He owned the Brinnon Store for 25 years. Balch married Hilda Sund of Lilliwaup, the daughter of early settlers who operated the well-known Sund's Resort.

New Organ for Schoolhouse. A team of oxen are used to deliver crates of supplies to the Hoh River School. There were few roads, and it was difficult to get in supplies. Sailing schooners from Port Townsend would bring supplies to a port or the mouth of a river, and depending upon the destination, the materials would be packed in on a man's back, by horseback, via a team of oxen, or brought up a river by canoe or boat.

Puncheon Trail. Big cedar logs split and laid down on stringers made a good trail for horses. The alternative was often mud all the way up to the horses' bellies.

Isaac Anderson Family. In 1891, Isaac Anderson homesteaded on the north side of the Hoh River about 3.5 miles from where it empties into the Pacific Ocean. In 1896, he met and married Maud Fletcher, whose family had settled that year a mile downstream on the south side of the river. They eventually had nine children. Isaac was a blacksmith who worked at many jobs to earn money, including maintaining horse trails and bridges, logging, fishing, and canning his beef for sale.

Hoh River Settlers, 1918. Pictured from left to right are (first row) baby Florence Northup, Mary Fletcher, and A. Henry Fletcher; (second row) Myrtle Anderson Northup, Maud Fletcher Anderson, Isaac Anderson, and Ben Northup.

Quilcene School Picnic, 1892. School districts in neighboring communities were invited to this picnic, hosted by the Quilcene School District. From left to right are Bob Ryan, Charlie Andrews, Claude Knight, Jack Ryan, Henry Knight, Malcolm O'Dell, a Mrs. Haus, Annie Hunter, driver for Tookey school delegation, Winnie Andres, Frances Tookey, Elva (Dolly Smith) Henderson, Thad Smith, Porter Smith, Channie Knight, Ana Edwards, U. G. Edwards, Allie Henderson, and Bob Henderson (standing).

The New Quilcene School, 1916. The school was said to be "one of the most modern in the State," according to the photographer, Paul M. Richardson.

LOGGING CREW. Many, if not most, homesteading men needed to spend time away from their farms to earn cash to buy necessities. Although food was raised on the land, it was necessary to buy matches, pipe tobacco, grain for animal feed, sugar, flour, oatmeal, kerosene, coffee beans, and clothing. Because the homestead law required continuous residency, these men left their wives and children on the claim to continue farming. Homesteaders were allowed to be away for six months out of a year.

Five

TREES

The Olympic Peninsula is home to vast forests of western hemlock, Sitka spruce, red cedar, Douglas fir, Pacific silver fir, and several other species. Sitka spruce and western hemlock can grow to tremendous size, reaching 300 feet in height and 23 feet in circumference. Nearly every bit of the spongy forest floor is taken up with living plants. Plants even live on others plants, giving the rain forest a moss-draped jungle-like appearance. Mosses, lichens, and ferns cover most everything, even rocks. Decaying plants provide space and nutrients for new pants. New trees sprout from fallen "nurse logs." Any clearings in the forest quickly become covered with vine maple, slide alder, and devil's club, making cross-country travel most challenging. The forest teems with animals, including Roosevelt elk, black-tailed deer, cougar, black bear, river otter, Olympic chipmunk, jumping mouse, marmot, and snow mole; and birds such as the varied thrush, western robin, winter wren, pileated woodpecker, gray jay, and junco; and insects, reptiles, and amphibians.

Beginning in the 1850s, timber on the Olympic Peninsula was logged at a feverish pace. Masts for ships and lumber for the constantly burning and rebuilding San Francisco provided early ready markets. Homesteaders cleared away the forest to make way for farmland. Investors from the east built most of the mills and financed many of the logging operations. What at first appeared to be a limitless resource was obviously not so. Conservationists feared that all of the trees would be cut or burned without efforts to rein in logging. Since 1897, millions of acres of the Olympic Peninsula's forested land bounced back and forth between those who would log the timber and those who would preserve it. Thanks to conservationists' efforts and three U.S. presidents, the Olympic National Park was created. Even so, the pace of harvesting accelerated as new equipment became available. Loggers who once used axes, saws, skid roads, and animal teams moved on to steam donkeys and railroads to pull the logs out of the woods. By the time log trucks and chainsaws came around, much of the forest had already been logged once.

Down a Skid Road. Pictured here is a logger riding a chain boat, or "pig," down a skid road.

Bringing Logs to the Beach. The Harry L. Brown logging outfit at Whitney Spit is pictured here.

Dragging Log Sections. On this skid road, horses and a driver were needed to keep the lumber moving.

Wooden Dosewallips Bridge. In August 1923, a steel truss Dosewallips River Bridge opened, extending Highway 101 over the Dosewallips River.

Moving Huge Logs. Loggers pose with a horse team about to drag logs over a skid road. At the end of the skid road the logs slid into the water, where they were amassed by the hundreds inside a floating barrier called a boom. Once floating, the raw timber could be towed by tugboat to a mill site.

Ox Team at Water's Edge. In the early years, draft animals provided the muscle to move logs to landings on a body of water, where they could be floated and towed to mills in rafts.

Oxen on a Skid Road. Once limbs were cut off, logs were sent down skid roads with the help of ox teams. Skid roads reached 2 miles, at most, into the forested hills and were made of logs placed across the trail. Dogfish liver oil was used to make the wood slick.

Snow Creek Logging Company Camp. The buildings would be moved to another camp site after all the trees in the area were cut.

The Bunk House. Pictured here are eight loggers at a Snow Creek Log Company camp at Discovery Bay. Note the caulked boots, pronounced "corked."

PAUSING TO POSE. A group of loggers sit in the cut of a tree. The two men on either end are standing on springboards. Loggers were divided into two camps: swampers and fallers. Swampers cut away underbrush so the fallers could get to the trees. Fallers worked in two-man teams cutting notches in the tree, driving in springboards on which to stand, and chopping and sawing until the tree fell.

Lumber Camp Cooks. From left to right are Bill Lundquist and Andy Martinsen. Written on the back: "Andy Martinsen, flunky in Ed Sims Dosewallips timber camp. Bill Lundquist, cook and old settler, cooked on tug boats worked by Captain Martinsen."

Tables Set for Hungry Loggers. The staff stands proudly in the background of the Snow Creek Log Company's dining hall.

Logging Camp Crew. The steam-powered donkey engine in the background and the railroad track were later versions of the horse and ox teams and the skid road.

Dance in the Woods. Four couples dance on a large, crosscut tree stump accompanied by a fiddle and mandolin. Hard work was balanced with play. Holidays, dances, sporting contests, and other community events provided opportunities to socialize and come together with people who shared the challenge of living in this remote corner of the country.

Bull Donkey and Logging Crew. The Bloedel Donavan Logging Company near Forks used a large steam engine, called a "bull donkey," that could pull huge loads. Train tracks replaced the skid roads, and the steam donkey replaced the horse and ox teams.

Flatcars on a Logging Trestle. This is the Snow Creek Logging Company at Blyn. Trestles were built from materials on hand and usually on a curve to add strength. When built on a straightaway, the flimsy contraptions would wobble.

STEAM DONKEY AND SPAR TREE. In the 1880s, steam-driven donkeys replaced horse and oxen power. Logs were moved using a system of cables and blocks pulled by the steam donkey engine.

Climax at Brinnon, 1895. The Climax was usually the preferred locomotive, especially on smaller operations with rough track.

Log Raft at Gettysburg. Many early logging railways terminated at log dumps along the coast where the timber could be sorted, formed into rafts, and then towed to mills. Coastal communities like Port Crescent, Gettysburg, Twin, and Pysht blossomed quickly but briefly.

Locomotive Pushing Flatcars of Logs. During the steam era, companies had their own logging railroads with countless miles of track. Logging railroads meant timber could be cut farther away from rivers, lakes, or the coast.

Tractor Pulling Flatcars of Logs. Logging roads enabled Northwest loggers to push farther inland from the coasts and rivers to supply the growing demand for lumber.

SMALL MILL IN THE WOODS. Lumber mills provided employment for early settlers who had to "prove up" their homesteads by building houses and working their land.

SHINGLE MILL AT QUILCENE. For a time, shingle mills were going full blast, employing men to make cedar shingles for export. When the supply of local cedar was used up, the mills shut down.

Railroad Extension over Water. Logs were moved on trains to ships or to be dumped into the water to float in log booms to sawmills.

Logs Floating in a Millpond. Waterfront sawmills turned huge logs into lumber. Big money came into the Northwest from the Midwest and farther east to build the mills and harvest the logs. Logging operations were often built entirely with outside capital, and the primary market for the lumber was also outside markets. Local sawmills easily supplied the needs of the Northwest settlers.

Big Blowdown. On January 29, 1921, gale force winds swept across the Olympic Peninsula, uprooting 6 billion feet of timber. It wiped out entire forest stands, blocked every road and highway to the West End, destroyed homes, and killed several thousand elk and countless other animals. Miraculously, there was no loss of human life. It took 125 men several weeks to clear the Olympic Loop Highway, blocked by as many as 300 trees per mile.

Port Discovery Mill. The S. L. Mastick Company of San Francisco established the mill and village where more than 300 people lived. Company vessels sailed away loaded with timber, and company housing and stores dotted the main street and hills along the bluff. By 1888, workers were cut to part-time, and the mill had new ownership in Moore and Smith, which eventually went bankrupt and sold its timber rights. The mill communities of Maynard, Fairmont, and Uncas became ghost towns.

Train under Discovery Bay Road, 1912. The Port Townsend Southern Railroad operated under eight different owners and two leases in its 94 years of operation, changing hands more times than any other railroad in the country. On August 22, 1998, some of the old railroad beds were dedicated as the Larry Scott Memorial Trail in the "Rails to Trails" initiative to give abandoned routes a new use for the future.

Snow Hiker, July 1909. Just about every high Olympic trail has some snow on it that lingers through July and well into August.

Six

Recreation

While indigenous people traditionally traveled into the Olympic Mountains to hunt elk and deer, the interior was almost totally unexplored until the 1890s. The steep peaks were an impenetrable wilderness cloaked in mystery. Local settlers and homesteaders roamed the range to hunt and fish while enjoying the high country's unsurpassed beauty. Most of these people left no records, but fortunately, some took photographs.

The first recorded exploration was led by U.S. Army lieutenant Joseph P. O'Neil beginning in 1885. In 1890, the *Seattle Press* expedition cartographer produced the first reasonably accurate map of the interior, which was part of a special 24-page edition of the *Seattle Press* on July 16, 1890. John Muir would later proclaim the need for preservation of this priceless wilderness after his own exploration in 1896. Federal management began in 1897 when Pres. Grover Cleveland issued a proclamation creating the Olympic Forest Reserve. Pres. Theodore Roosevelt established the Mount Olympus National Monument in 1909 to help preserve forest and grazing areas for the native elk population. In 1938, Pres. Franklin D. Roosevelt officially established Olympic National Park as a protected area under control of the U.S. Department of Interior's National Park Service.

The Olympics were an early destination for intrepid adventurers. Majestic mountains, vast glaciers, and wilderness trails have long lured hikers and climbers. First arriving by boat, then by combination of boat and automobile, visitors came to enjoy the rivers, pristine lakes, diverse wildlife, and old-growth forests.

No roads penetrate far into the interior, although a network of hiking trails was established early. The Civilian Conservation Corp (CCC) was a work-relief program created by Pres. Franklin D. Roosevelt in 1933 that put workers—mostly young, destitute men—into military-style bands of crews to build infrastructure on public lands. Beginning in the summer of 1933, five CCC camp crews planted trees and constructed roads, trails, bridges, campgrounds, firebreaks, telephone lines, backcountry shelters, buildings, and other projects in the Olympic National Park that are still enjoyed today.

THE VIEW ABOVE THE VALLEY MIST. The weather in the Olympics is extremely unpredictable. On the summit this hiker can watch the weather change.

DUNNING FAMILY HIKE. Kate Dunning wrote in an account of a vacation in the Olympic Mountains in August 1912, "the sight [at the summit] was beautiful. Below us on one side lay ridges and ridges of mountains, further Hoods Canal and Puget Sound, then the forts and Protection Island, then on the other side an even more wonderful sight met our eyes—far below us was as an ocean of clouds, with peaks sticking out here and there like small islands. It was perfectly wonderful, and everyone who has never been above the clouds can't begin to appreciate how wonderful it is."

Boy Scouts on Iron Mountain, 1914. Robert Marriott recalled in his oral history that Boy Scouts hiking in the Olympics had different degrees of stamina. "Some would be way up ahead and others would be dragging back." But no matter what the degree of stamina, there was always a place that became "Poop-out Drag," where the hike caught up with the boys. "In those days we didn't have the fancy packboards that they have now. We just had old rucksacks from World War I; hobnail boots from World War I were standard equipment."

SUMMIT OF IRON MOUNTAIN, 1929. Many were convinced that the Olympics would inevitably yield riches as great as those of the California and Klondike gold rushes. Hundreds of claims were filed on Iron Mountain alone. To date, no mineral deposits warranting the effort of extraction have been found.

ENJOYING THE SCENERY. In most areas of the Olympics the solitude and primitive wilderness experience of the early exploring parties is beyond the reach of day hikers. Packers served as tour guides for early tourists venturing deep into the mountains. Today nearly 200 miles of trails in the Olympic National Park are maintained for hikers using horses, burrows, and llamas as pack animals.

Fording the Lillian River. One of the first expeditions to explore the Olympics in the 1880s had little more than started when it met disaster. After crossing a large stream, the pack animals lost their footing, and the equipment and supplies were swept away by the river.

Crossing at Low Water. A pack train crosses the Hoh River near Spruce in this photograph.

Minnie Peterson, "The Packer." Peterson's 50-year packing career began when her husband, Oscar, asked if she would help with the pack horses during hunting season. Although she had four small children, Minnie took to leading trails of horses through the wilderness. Eventually she and Oscar bought a string of pack horses and led trips for other groups, including the Sierra Club. A campground, the Minnie Peterson Camp and Picnic Area, sits along the Hoh River 9 miles south of Forks.

Pack Train on Mountain Trail. Camping with pack animals that could easily carry large tents, warm and comfortable bedding, and plenty of food made "roughing it" far more pleasant. It also greatly increased the range of campers.

On the Glacier, Mount Constance. At 7,743 feet, this is the third-highest peak in the Olympic Mountains. Many of the routes are exposed and hazardous. Despite the hazards, Mount Constance remains a popular climbing spot. Olympic Mountain Rescue (OMR) was formed after a World War II climbing boom. Prior to that, climbing was a sport with a select few participants, who were generally well experienced. In the late 1940s and early 1950s, there were a number of climbing accidents in the Olympics, including fatalities on both Mount Anderson and Mount Olympus.

Scouts in the Snow, 1914. The Boy Scouts have a long history with the Olympics. A group of scouts climbed into the Mount Olympus area in 1914, prior to the organization of local Scout councils. This photograph was taken by George Welch. Two years later, while climbing Mount Olympus, Welch took a fall. He was not injured by the fall, but his pack landed on him and broke his back. "It took two days to haul him out of the mountains," his granddaughter Ann Welch reported. "They thought that he might not be able to walk again." But he did, although it took him a year. The photographs start again in 1918 and continue through 1923.

HEADWATERS OF THE HOH RIVER. The Hoh River is fed from glaciers surrounding Mount Olympus. Snowmelt and silt make for a cold, milk-colored river. The river and its valley provide habitat for the endangered northern spotted owl, marbled murrelet, Pacific Chinook salmon, and wild steelhead.

Bird Hunting. This postcard is postmarked October 8, 1903. The note from Paul Richardson said, "Was out hunting yesterday and you see the results. PR."

Duck Hunting. The Olympic Peninsula leads Washington State in both winter and spring bird counts. This postcard is postmarked December 14, 1908. The note from Paul Richardson on the back said, "Dear Ralph, Got a letter from Ivan yesterday and he is now married. Took all of us off our feet when we heard it. This was out at our reserve yesterday. PR."

Hunting Dog. This postcard is postmarked January 27, 1909. Paul Richardson's note on the back reads, "Dear Bro., You bet I will be on deck for Sunday if it don't storm too hard. Ever Yours, PR."

Elk in an Alpine Snowfield. In 1909, Pres. Theodore Roosevelt established the Mount Olympus National Monument to protect the summer range and breeding grounds of the Olympic elk, which were later renamed Roosevelt elk. These animals became endangered as a result of their popularity as the mascot of the fraternal order Benevolent and Protective Order of Elks (BPOE). Members of this organization used elk teeth as ornaments in their watch fobs. Roosevelt elk are the largest breed of elk, with a powerful physique that enables them to swim, break through deep snow, and climb into high elevations.

John Huelsdonk with Cougar Skins. John Huelsdonk (1867–1946) came to the Olympic Peninsula in 1892. He was the first settler to homestead on the Hoh River, about 30 miles up the valley. Short of stature with a massive torso and powerful arms, he was known as "the Iron Man of the Hoh." Huelsdonk had to pack everything miles up a rough mountain trail that forded streams on narrow logs. He became famous as a trapper and hunter, having killed more than 200 cougars.

George Lomsdalen, Bounty Hunter. Hunters used dogs to find and chase wildcats up trees, where they were easy to finish off with a rifle. In the early 1900s, the elk population in the Olympics was dwindling because of overhunting and too many predators. In 1904, the State of Washington set a bounty on cougars. A newspaper article in a July 1905 *Port Townsend Leader* announced, "Bounty will be paid for wild animals." Many called this bounty their "cash crop." The annual harvest ran from 40 to 250 cougars. In 1930, *Port Townsend Leader* headlines included, "Seven wildcats brought Bounty here last week," "Bounty paid on five cats last week," "Four wildcats brought in for county bounty," "Tarboo men get second big Cougar," "Cougar shot out of tree at Quilcene," "Hoofs of deers found in Cougars stomach," and "West Ender gets $85 in Wild animal bounties." The 1940s were the peak cougar bounty hunting years. The bounty was repealed in 1961.

Hunting Camp. Chester Twitchell of Leland (right) and an unidentified fellow hunter are pictured here.

Successful Hunt. Outdoor recreation such as hunting and fishing often blurred the lines between work and play.

After the Hunt. Pictured here is the packing out of the photographer's deer. The back of this postcard reads, "Bringing in the buck Paul killed."

Fishing on the Hoh. In some places the Hoh River can be waded, but it remains a dangerous river. Cold water, strong currents, and unstable log jams await the incautious.

LAURA BRYANT FISHING. The Olympic Peninsula provided even the Victorian lady with sporting opportunities.

FISHING A WILD RIVER. The Olympic National Park, with its abundant rainfall and snowy mountains, hundreds of lakes and streams, 10 major rivers, and the Pacific Ocean, provides habitat for 37 species of native fish.

HORACE MCCURDY FISHING. H. W. McCurdy was born in Port Townsend on July 30, 1899, the son of one of the city's best-known families. He grew up to be a ship and bridge builder. His firm, Puget Sound Bridge and Dredging, built the Lake Washington Floating Bridge in 1940 and the Hood Canal Floating Bridge in 1961.

LADIES FISHING. Some of the best fishing in the world can still be found on the Elwha, Bogachiel, Hoh, and Sol Duc Rivers and at Lake Leland, Lake Aldwell, Lake Sutherland, Lake Crescent, Lake Pleasant, and Lake Ozette.

Salmon Catch, c. 1922. Elizabeth Gawbee caught this fine fish on the Dungeness River near Sequim.

EUGENE BEST'S DOSEWALLIPS CATCH. Willard and Cornelia Best left New York City for the West in the spring of 1898 with their two small children, Eugene and Dora. They found their way to Brinnon in 1908, arriving with four more children.

Civilized Tent Camping. The McCurdy family knew how to set up a comfortable camp. Anna Laursen McCurdy cooks as Horace McCurdy watches. The photographer, James G. McCurdy, took hundreds of wonderful photographs.

A Pair of Olympic Marmots. The wildlife is one of the joys of camping. Marmots are the most social and gregarious mammals on the peninsula. They live in burrows and hibernate through the winter. Most are highly social and use loud whistles to communicate with one another, especially when alarmed. Olympic marmots are found nowhere else in the world.

Wilcox Campsite. Automobiles made going out into the woods easier and created the need for all kinds of camp sites.

Lake Family Campsite. Sanford Lake drove his family to this campsite, taking photographs along the way.

EDGAR SIMS AND JOHN SIEBENBAUM CAMPING. Both were prominent Port Townsend businessmen who loved getting out into the woods. Sims (right) made his fortune with salmon canneries and served in the state legislature. There, he was instrumental in securing funds for the Olympic Loop Highway. Siebenbaum, active in many business ventures, built Port Townsend's First American National Bank Building, the Siebenbaum Building, and the Buhler Motor Company building, all of which are still standing.

Roughing It at Camp Crackerville. George Welch and P. M. Richardson were avid outdoorsmen who camped, hiked, hunted, and took photographs in the Olympics before World War I. Welch was an early advocate for the creation of the Olympic National Park and used his photography and a letter-writing campaign in that effort.

A Simple Camp. A tarp, ropes, and blankets made a fine camp, if it did not rain. On the west side of the Olympic Mountains the average rainfall is almost 180 inches. To the east, many areas are quite dry, especially in the summer.

Cooking over a Beach Fire. With such an abundance of shellfish and firewood, clam bakes and beach picnics were, and still are, popular waterfront activities.

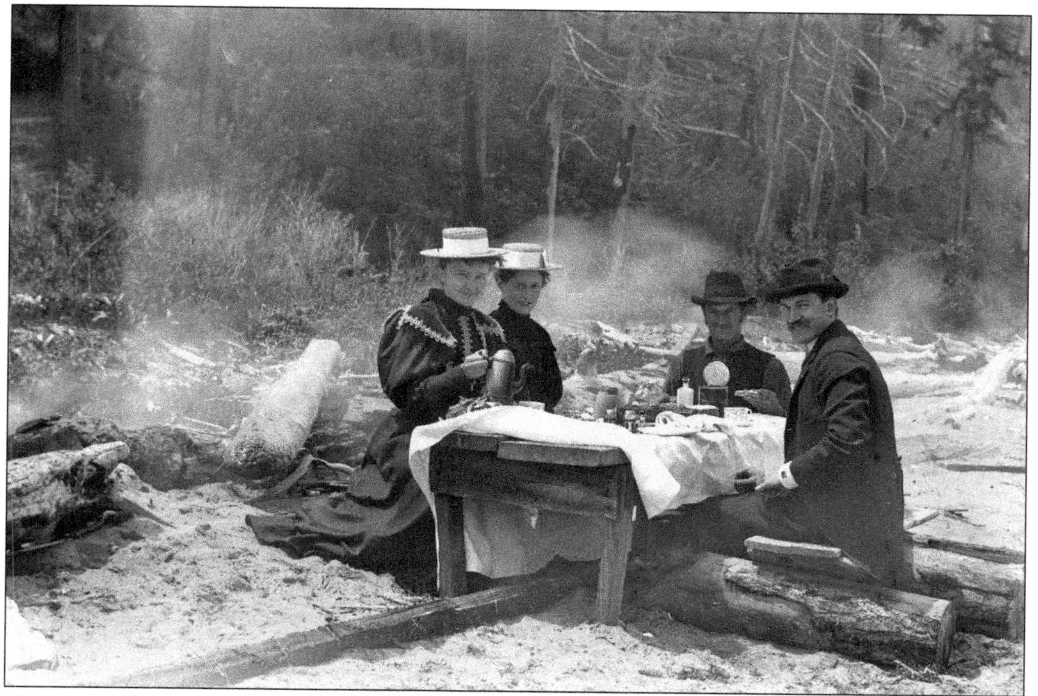

Civilized Picnicking. Anna (left) and James McCurdy (right) and an unidentified couple picnicked on the beach with linen and china.

McArdle Family on Quilcene Bay. This bay on Hood Canal is famous for its oysters, clams, shrimp, crab, and fish.

Dunning Family on Ocean Beach. This family farmed in Quilcene, quite a trek around the mountains on bumpy dirt roads to reach the Pacific Coast.

EXPLORING THE BEACH, 1910. Two children, possibly Rosetta Klocker and Horace McCurdy, explored a rocky beach at low tide. Note the sailing ship in the background.

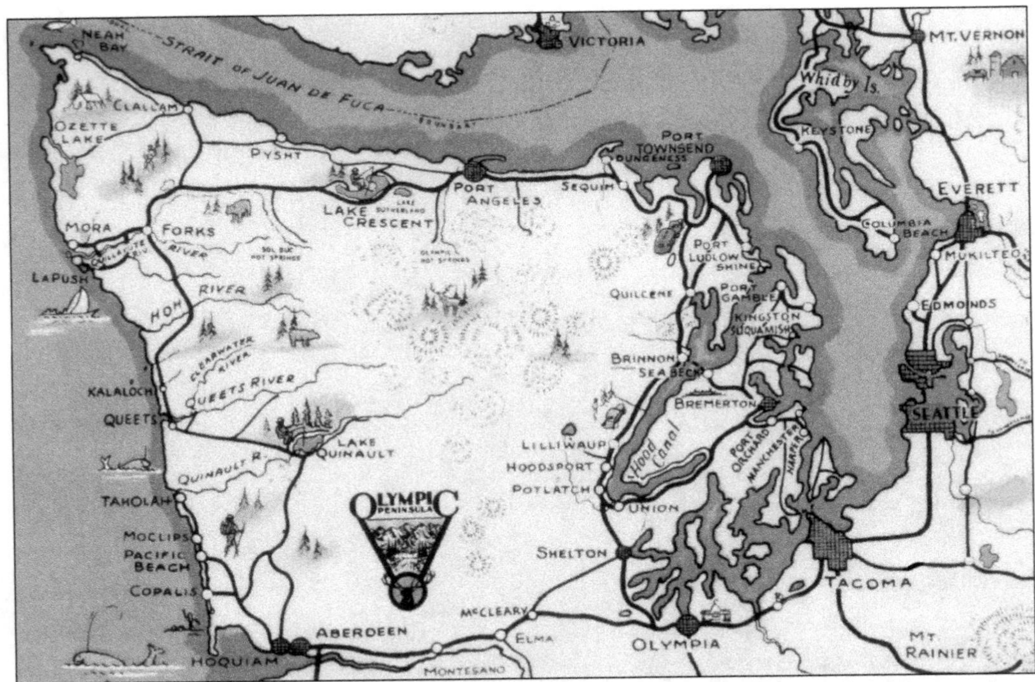

Map of the Olympic Peninsula. The Olympic Loop (Highway 101) opened the peninsula to tourism. The loop is approximately 330 miles in distance and, nowadays, can be driven in a day.

Admiring the View. As elsewhere in the United States, the Ford Model T was a common purchase. Affordable, tough, and easy to fix, the Model T could travel on rough roads and was even put to work on the farm. Henry Ford is credited with encouraging the five-day work week so his workers would have time to enjoy the cars he sold them.

Seven

The Loop

Despite its remote location and lack of roads, the automobile and truck took root in the Olympic Peninsula during World War I, when farmers and loggers were enjoying a brief period of prosperity. More car owners created a demand for more roads, which began to appear in the 1920s and 1930s. Progress was slow; soils were usually unstable, and thick underbrush was everywhere. For many years intrepid car owners negotiated single-lane, unpaved roads.

Completed in 1931 at a cost of $10 million, the Olympic Loop Highway (currently Highway 101) is a 330-mile-long circle around the Olympic Mountains. The new road made this beautiful but remote area accessible to tourism for the first time. The many existing resorts and campgrounds adapted to serve the auto tourist. Advertisements for hotels, health spas, and Native American villages—all within driving distance from Seattle and the nearest ferry—boasted of every convenience.

One Olympic Peninsula postcard booklet from the 1930s said:

> Surrounding a great mountain range, the Olympic Highway Loop forms a circle tour of unusual interest and scenic attractions. . . . Along Hood Canal, through the Olympic National Forest, around historic Discovery Bay, past Lake Sutherland and Lake Crescent, down the seacoast to Lake Quinault and the Grays Harbor ocean beaches; then through the harbor cities and on to the state capitol at Olympia, the trip around the Olympic Highway Loop is an outstanding Pacific Coast motor tour.

And the 1949 directory, *Visit the Olympic Peninsula*, published by the Olympic Peninsula Resort and Hotel Association, read:

> The magnificent Olympic Peninsula in the extreme "upper left-hand" corner of the United States is truly America's Last Frontier. In this scenic paradise are areas not yet reached by white man; wildernesses so forbidding only the very hardy dare venture near. Yet a great many parts of this rugged country are easily accessible by automobile and boat—just a short ride from metropolitan centers.

Opening the Loop. The opening celebration for the Olympic Loop Highway at the Kalaloch Creek Bridge on August 26, 1931, included marching bands and Native Americans. Members of five coastal tribes, the Quillayutes, Quinaults, Queets, Hoh, and Makah held contests and performed traditional games and dances to mark the occasion. The Seattle Chamber of Commerce led a caravan of business people from Port Angeles to Kalaloch, dedicating various bridges en route.

Some Cars at the Opening. Motorists enthusiastically attended the celebration of the opening of Highway 101, the Olympic Highway Loop. About 6,000 people participated in the two-day gala opening.

Motoring through the Big Trees. Even before the loop was completed, motorists set out to explore the beautiful Olympic Peninsula forests.

MOTORING ON THE OLYMPIC HIGHWAY. In the 1920s and 1930s, increasing numbers of car owners provided the impetus for road building on the Olympic Peninsula. Progress on road construction, however, was slow. For many years, car owners negotiated single-lane, unpaved roads, or worse.

QUEEN HOTEL, QUILCENE. The Queen Hotel was one of the earliest guest accommodations in the area.

LOG CABIN INN, QUILCENE. Charlie and Laura Beck owned and operated the Log Cabin Inn near the fish hatchery at Penny Creek from about 1910 to 1934. The fish hatchery, originally constructed in 1911, raised coho, chum, pink, Chinook, and sockeye salmon and brook, cutthroat, and rainbow trout for visitors to the inn (and many other places) to catch.

Linger Longer Lodge Veranda. *The Megaphone* newspaper office and its waterwheel are in the background. Brandon and Jessie Satterlee turned a 40-acre homestead into a popular summer resort. Jessie is credited with creating the poetic name.

Linger Longer Lodge Dining Room. This waterfront resort started with the pioneer Linconfelter home in Quilcene. It was constructed of native material with a rustic décor. The lodge and cabins could accommodate 125 guests. In 1922, the Linger Longer Lodge charged $4 per night, meals included, with even lower rates for those who lingered longer. The lodge was twice destroyed by fire; first in 1928 and again in 1959.

ALONG HOOD CANAL. Brinnon and Quilcene are small towns nestled along scenic Hood Canal on the eastern edge of the Olympic National Forest. Here, Roosevelt elk migrate along the Dosewallips, Duckabush, and Hamma Hamma Rivers. In the spring, the elk are often visible from the highway, wandering the tide flats and foraging in salt marshes.

AUTOMOBILE WITH "TOWNSEND" BANNER. The City of Port Townsend collected annual license fees for automobiles and issued fines to anyone caught diving without a license. In Washington State, driver licensing was started in 1921. Applicants were required to furnish the signatures of two people who would state that the person was a competent driver and had no physical problems that would impair safe driving. Driving examinations were not initiated until 1937.

WILLIAM H. WILCOX AT THE WHEEL. Wilcox was the private secretary to the Port Townsend collector of customs from 1897 until the customs office closed. He moved to Seattle in 1914. Wilcox was an ardent photographer and friend and neighbor of another Port Townsend photographer, James G. McCurdy.

The Whistling Oyster. An "up-class" dining facility and hotel, the "Whistling O" burned down in 1944. It was immediately rebuilt and is still in its original location at the junction of U.S. Highway 101 and Linger Longer Road.

Whistling Oyster Lobby, before 1944. Until recently, the bar was the home of the Grand Masters Shuffleboard Tournament.

MOTORING DOWN A COUNTRY ROAD. The popularity of automobiles brought about the demand for roads and vice versa.

MAPLES STORE AT BRINNON. The store was owned and run by W. R. and Donalia Frey in the 1930s.

BRINNON BRIDGE, 1915. The Sanford Lake family was on their first long trip in "El Diablo."

Pierce's Resort on Hood Canal. Clint Pierce and his wife, Margaret, turned the old Tom Pierce place into a resort around 1912. Of Pierce's Resort, Douglas Egan said, "I can remember the great food, fried chicken and steaks and vegetable from their garden and thick cream from their dairy. There was no electricity. I remember the oil lamps and candles. Making ice cream was an event. They would have us kids turning the crank."

Wildwood Inn and Auto Camp. When the Wildwood opened, the Olympic Loop Highway had just been completed. Most families in the Quilcene area owned automobiles and enjoyed the good chicken dinners and rustic charm of the restaurant. The camp offered tourists a filling station, a restaurant, three double cabins, and three single cabins.

Macomber's in Brinnon. This combination post office, store, and hotel was a local gathering place until it burned down sometime before 1918.

Cottage Inn, Brinnon, 1930s. The message on the back of this postcard reads, "We are camping in front of tourist hotel now. Going up to Rocky Brooks tomorrow. Were up beyond Duckabush."

Olympic Hot Springs in the Snow. Until 1930, when a road was completed, these springs were accessible only by foot or horseback. The resort boasted a log hotel, a pool, and cabins. It operated until 1966, when the lease expired. Heavy winter snows caused many of the old buildings to collapse. The buildings were removed, but the hot springs remain. The Olympic hot springs consist of 21 seeps along a bank of Boulder Creek, a tributary of the Elwha River. Several have been fashioned into rock-lined pools about a foot deep. Water temperatures vary from lukewarm to 138 degrees Fahrenheit (54 degrees Celsius).

Lake Crescent, July 4, 1915. Before the Olympic highway was extended along the lake's south shore in 1922, travelers took the ferryboat from the East Beach dock on their way to the forests and ocean beaches of the peninsula.

Big Expedition. Pictured here is the visit of the Seattle Chamber of Commerce to Forks on July 4, 1919.

GRAYS MARSH HUNTING LODGE. Although promoted as a port city on the Strait of Juan de Fuca, Port Williams failed to survive.

THE MERRY RESORT. This tourist accommodation near Port Angeles was creatively built with local logs.

VIEWS OF LAKE QUINAULT LODGE. The original log hotel was constructed in 1896. In 1923, fire destroyed the hotel, but it was rebuilt in 1926 at a cost of $90,000. Some of the Northwest's premier craftsmen worked on the project, which entailed hauling supplies 50 miles over a dirt road. The most famous visitor in the lodge's history was Pres. Franklin D. Roosevelt in 1937. Roosevelt came to study the feasibility of a national park in the area, and the next year he signed legislation to create the Olympic National Park.

Ruby Beach Resort. Built by John and Elizabeth Fletcher, the resort had a store, restaurant, and cabins off the road and on the beach. The U.S. government took it over during World War II to house military personnel assigned to coast defense. While the resort is gone, the beach remains one of the most scenic on the coast, with rugged sea stacks, flat sand, and a small stream.

Sol Duc Hotel. Michael Earles opened his Sol Duc Hot Springs Resort in 1912. It was a 164-room, five-star hotel and resort that drew thousands of visitors from as far away as Europe. The Hot Springs Company provided transportation to this remote area. The Sol Duc steamer picked up passengers in Seattle, Port Townsend, Port Williams, Dungeness, and Port Angeles and took them to Port Crescent. Automobiles would pick up the groups and transport them to East Beach. Here a steam launch would take the visitors to Fairholme at the west end of the lake. A Stanley steamer provided the final leg of the journey to the resort.

Glass Floats at Ruby Beach. Glass floats that Japanese fishermen once used to support their nets were part of the flotsam and jetsam cast upon the beach. It took the ocean currents about a year to carry the floats across the Pacific Ocean to the Washington coast. Elizabeth "Missy" Fletcher Barlow became a well-known artist whose work captures the wilderness spirit of the western Olympic Peninsula.

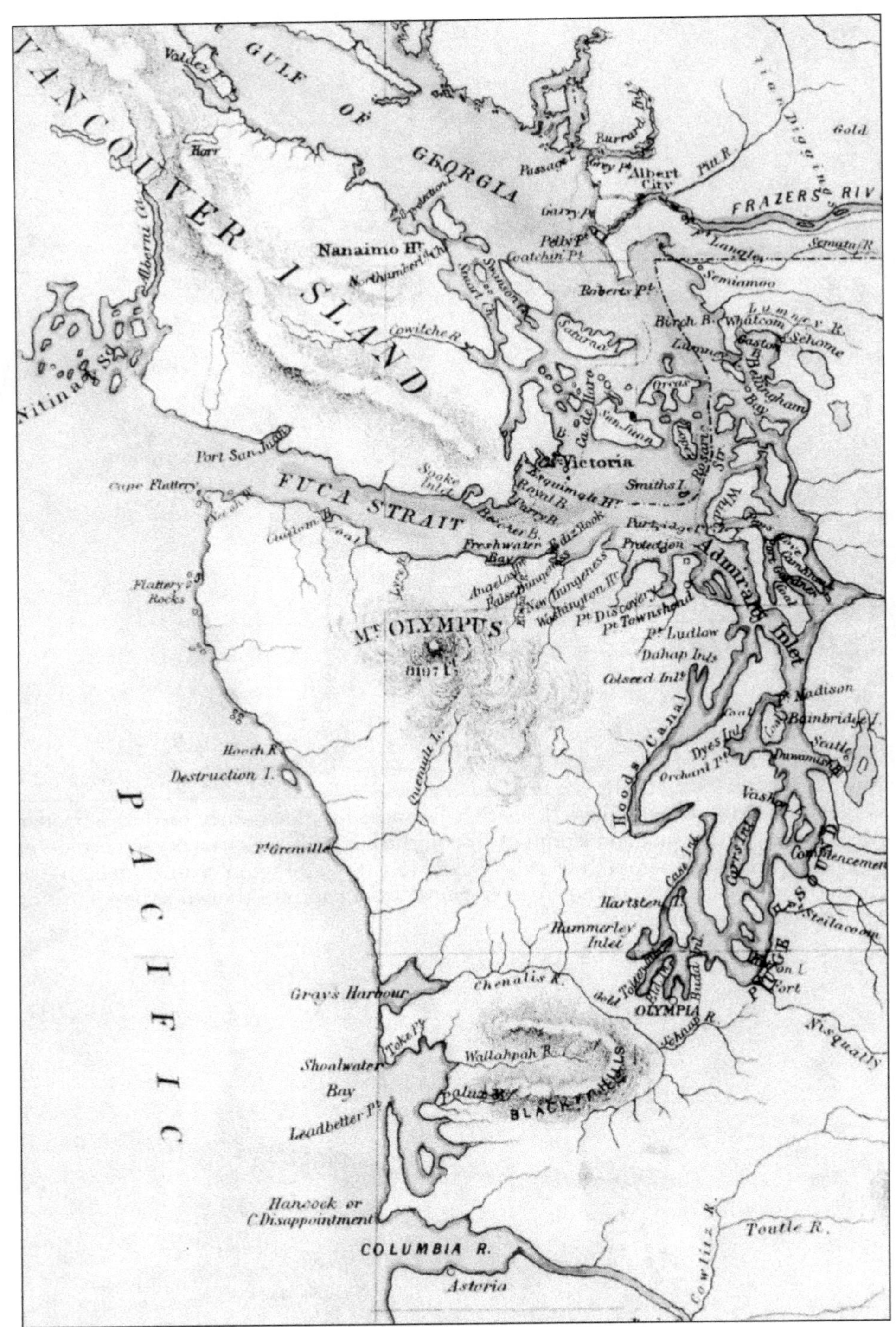

Early Olympic Peninsula Map. The Pacific Ocean is to the west, the Strait of Juan de Fuca is to the north, and Admiralty Inlet, Puget Sound, and Hood Canal flow in and around the east. Mount Olympus rises near the center of the peninsula, the highest point in the Olympic Mountains.

Bibliography

Bailey, Ida and Vern. *A Scrapbook of History Brinnon*. Bremerton, WA: Perry Publishing, 1997.

Bergland, Eric O. and Jerry Marr. *Prehistoric Life on the Olympic Peninsula: The First Inhabitants of a Great American Wilderness*. Seattle, WA: Pacific Northwest National Parks and Forests Association, 1988.

El Hult, Ruby. *Untamed Olympics: The Story of a Peninsula*. Portland, OR: Binfords and Mort, Publishers, 1954.

Fletcher, Elizabeth Huelsdonk. *The Iron Man of the Hoh: The Man Not the Myth*. Port Angeles, WA: Creative Communications, 1979.

Hermanson, James. *Rural Jefferson County: Its Heritage and Maritime History*. Port Townsend, WA, 2001.

www.jamestowntribe.org

Jefferson County Historical Society. *Charles Azel Anderson, A Hoh River Man for All Season*. Port Townsend, WA: Jefferson County Historical Society Oral History Project, 1989.

———. *Elizabeth Huelsdonk Fletcher, A Pioneer's Daughter*. Port Townsend, WA: Jefferson County Historical Society Oral History Project, 1989.

———. *Myrtle May Anderson Northup: Memories of Early Days on the Hoh and Clearwater Rivers*. Port Townsend, WA: Jefferson County Historical Society Oral History Project, 1989.

———. *William Edward Matheson: Reminiscences of a Hadlock Man*. Port Townsend, WA: Jefferson County Historical Society Oral History Project, 1989.

———. *With Pride in Heritage: History of Jefferson County*. Port Townsend, WA: 1966.

Lein, Carsten. *Exploring the Olympic Mountains: Accounts of the Earliest Expeditions 1878–1890*. Seattle, WA: The Mountaineers Books, 2001.

www.lostresort.net

McClary, Daryl C. *Members of the Olympic Exploring Expedition Make First Recorded Ascent of Mount Olympus on September 22, 1890*: Seattle, WA: HistoryLink.org, September 20, 2005.

Morgan, Murray. *The Last Wilderness*. New York: The Viking Press, 1955.

Olympic Mountain Rescue. *Olympic Mountains: A Climbing Guide*. Seattle, WA: The Mountaineers Books, 2006.

www.olympic.national-park.com

Parratt, Smitty. *Gods and Goblins: A Field Guide to Place Names of Olympic National Park*. Port Angeles, WA: CP Publications, Inc., 1984.

www.ptleader.com

Swan, James G. *Almost Out of the World: Scenes in Washington Territory*. Tacoma, WA: Washington State Historical Society, 1971.

www.voluntaryist.com

www.washington.edu/uwired/outreach

Watner, Carl. *The Precursor of National Identification Cards in the U.S.: Drivers Licenses and Vehicle Registration in Historical Perspective*.

Wood, Robert L. *The Land That Slept Late: The Olympic Mountains in Legend and History*. Seattle, WA: The Mountaineers, 1995.

CPSIA information can be obtained
at www.ICGtesting.com
Printed in the USA
LVHW101510261020
669854LV00013B/618